A GUIDE
IN THE WILDERNESS

WILLIAM COOPER

A GUIDE
IN THE WILDERNESS

OR THE

HISTORY OF THE FIRST SETTLEMENTS

IN THE

WESTERN COUNTIES OF NEW YORK

WITH

USEFUL INSTRUCTIONS TO FUTURE SETTLERS ·

IN A SERIES OF LETTERS ADDRESSED BY JUDGE
WILLIAM COOPER, OF COOPERSTOWN, TO
WILLIAM SAMPSON, BARRISTER, OF
NEW YORK.

 BOOKS FOR LIBRARIES PRESS
FREEPORT, NEW YORK

First Published 1810
Reprinted 1970

INTERNATIONAL STANDARD BOOK NUMBER:
0-8369-5595-1

LIBRARY OF CONGRESS CATALOG CARD NUMBER:
79-140352

PRINTED IN THE UNITED STATES OF AMERICA

A GUIDE IN THE WILDERNESS; or the History of the First Settlement in the Western Counties of New York, with useful Instructions to Future Settlers. In a series of letters address by JUDGE COOPER, of COOPERS-TOWN, to William Sampson, Barrister, of New York. Dublin: printed by Gilbert & Hodges, 27 Dame Street. 1810.

Three hundred copies printed, 1897, with an Introduction by James Fenimore Cooper, for George P. Humphrey, Rochester, N. Y.

"The place (Cooperstown) was founded by one man, William Cooper, whose recorded experiences of pioneering, remain a gem in the literature of the State."—Doctor Margaret Louise Plunkett, Assistant in American History, Cornell University; History of State of New York. Vol. VIII, page 60.

INTRODUCTION

William Cooper, the writer of the letters composing the "Guide in the Wilderness" was born December 2, 1754, in Byberry township, then in Philadelphia county, Pennsylvania. He married December 12, 1775, at Burlington, New Jersey, Elizabeth Fenimore, daughter of Richard Fenimore, a descendant of early English settlers in New Jersey. He became interested in large tracts of land in New York and elsewhere shortly after the Revolution, and from that time, until his death in 1809, his principal occupation seems to have been settling his own lands and those in which he had a joint interest with others.

The time was one of great activity in land settlement and speculation. Few, if any, new settlements had been undertaken during the war and this period of stagnation was naturally followed by large speculative purchases of wild lands by men with money to invest. The rapidity with which land could be disposed of to persons seeking homes is shown by the settlement of the tract of which the village of Cooperstown forms a part. Judge Cooper after examining his land in 1785 offered forty thousand acres for sale to settlers, and he states, that in sixteen days it was all taken up by the poorer class of people, who bought principally small holdings. Here, at the foot of Otsego lake, in 1787, he laid out a village which was given the name of Coopers-Town. He gradually acquired other large tracts of land in the neighborhood, and had, practically, the management of the settlement of the greater part of what is now Otsego county, either as owner or by agreement with the owners, as well as of lands in other parts of the state which he owned or controlled.

Speculation in American lands was not confined to residents of this country. Large tracts were bought by foreigners. The voluminous correspondence which Judge Cooper has left shows that Necker, and afterwards Madame de Stael, were owners of lands in our northern counties. Under the stimulus of this speculation land in some localities brought prices which it is doubtful if it has realized since. Judge Cooper paid ten dollars an acre for land in what is now known as the North Woods, which is hardly worth a quarter of that price to-day. Generally, however, his judgment was remarkably good. This is shown by his designation in one of the following letters of the locations which were likely, in his opinion, to become important towns; among them he mentions the mouth of the Buffalo creek—now Buffalo; the straits of Niagara below the falls—now Lewiston, and the first falls of the Genesee—now Rochester.

When the "Guide in the Wilderness" was written, the only means of transportation were waterways and roads; and the value of lands, present and future, rested largely on their location with reference to rivers and lakes, to roads or the probable line of great highways. Already a canal was under discussion and the suggestions on this subject of Judge Cooper are interesting in view of the subsequent building of the Erie Canal. One element in the speculative value of land, which investors apparently overlooked, was the effect which the clearing of the forests would have on the streams. Large tracts of land, then deemed valuable because they were located on the banks of some stream, navigable for scows and small boats, soon lost the advantage of such a location by the shrinking of the streams, due to the cutting away of the woods.

Great profits were anticipated from the manufacture of maple sugar, and among Cooper's papers is a copy of a letter to the President of the United States (George Washington) which accompanied a present of "sugar and spirits produced from the maple tree" sent by Arthur Noble (after whom the patents of Arthurboro and Noble-boro are named) and Judge Cooper.

The views of the author of the "Guide" on the wisdom of selling in fee, instead of leasing in fee, have been proved sound, by the collapse of the attempt to create in this State a system of land proprietorship based on per-petual leases binding the tenants to the payment of perpet-ual rent. This course was followed on many of the great estates in New York and resulted in endless litigation and the "anti-rent war".

Life, in what was then the frontier settlement of Cooperstown, was not without its interests other than those of mere business. The village grew and the settlers in the surrounding country prospered. In 1790 Judge Cooper brought his family from Burlington. It consisted of fifteen persons, including servants. In the same year, as appears from a census taken then, the village proper contained eight families with a total of thirty-three persons and two slaves; seven houses and three barns. This "census" is endorsed by the maker as follows: "I may not be perfectly correct, but the difference is not material if any." In 1802 the population had increased to 342 whites and 7 blacks, and in 1816 to 826 persons. Churches, an "academy" and a public library had been started. A newspaper was published in 1795, and at least one has been published in the village continuously since. Cooperstown at the time of the writing of the "Guide in the Wilderness" stood in point of trade and population next to Utica. The former now has about 2900 inhabitants and the latter about 45,000.

Jacob Morris, writing in January 1796, says: "The brilliancy exhibited at Cooperstown last Tuesday—the Masonic festival—was the admiration and astonishment of all beholders. Upwards of eighty people sat down to one table—some very excellent toasts were drank and the greatest decency and decorum was observed. . . . . In the evening we had a splendid ball, sixty couple, thirty in a set, both sets on the floor at the same time, pleasant manners and good dancing."

This was not the first ball given at Cooperstown. There is the record of the trial, in 1791, of a Doctor P., who was charged with having mixed an emetic with the beverage drunk at a ball given at the "Red Lion." He was tried, convicted of the offense, put in the stocks, and then banished from the village. Banishment was not an unusual, though probably an unlawful form of punishment at the time.

The place seems to have been attractive to foreigners, seeking a permanent or temporary home in this country, as many of them found their way to it. For some years an ex-governor* of one of the French islands kept a shop in the village. Talleyrand visited Judge Cooper, and wrote verses to one of his daughters, and many of the prominent federalists of the state stayed for longer or shorter periods with him. In 1796 he began a large brick house for his own occupation calling it Otsego Hall. It took the place of an older one known as the Mansion. Here open house was kept and a liberal hospitality dispensed. Traveling was done by short stages, over poor roads, from the home of one friend or acquaintance to that of another, and doubtless the Mansion, and later the Hall, received their share of such patronage. Traditions still live of the good times enjoyed, and the receipted bills for the tuns of madeira consumed have long survived the giver and partakers of the feasts. That dinners were not unusual is apparent from the following provision in the lease of Judge Cooper's house, made in 1798, when he went to Philadelphia for the winter but expected to board with the lessee at times: "When he makes a dinner for his friends, then the said William shall pay three shillings per man to the said Samuel and on all occasions find his own liquors."

The hospitality, if tradition speaks truly, was sometimes enforced with amiable roughness. The story is still told of how Judge Cooper, while driving a sleigh full of guests, stopped at the house of a friend, an ex-officer of the French army,† who was living on the shores of Otsego lake, and asked him to join the party and dine at the Hall. He firmly declined the invitation, but his would-be entertainers were not to be discouraged and carried him forcibly to the dinner. Arrived at the Hall they found, to their delight, that their captive, suffering from the delays and inconveniences of frontier housekeeping, was without a shirt. Judge Cooper, however, supplied him with one, and, as the involuntary guest was frequently heard to say afterwards, was so hospitable as to give him a ruffled one.

---

*He went by the name of "F. Z. LeQuoy," and had been Civil Governor of Martinique, but was called "de Mersereau" by a fellow countryman who had known him while Governor. He returned to, and died of yellow fever, at Martinique.

† L'Abbé de Raffcourt.

The head of a settlement was subject to other demands than those on his wardrobe. One of the French settlers borrowed of Judge Cooper some fifty dollars. As time went on the latter noticed that his debtor's visits to the Hall became less and less frequent until they finally ceased. Meeting the man one day, he remonstrated with him, telling him that so small a matter should not cause him annoyance and urging him not to allow it to interfere with his visits to the Hall. The Frenchman, however, felt that the fifty dollars weighed heavily on his honor, and that he could not partake of the Judge's hospitality until the debt was paid. Not long afterwards Judge Cooper saw his debtor approaching him with every manifestation of joy, waving his hat and shouting: "Good news! Judge Cooper! My mother is dead! I pay you the fifty dollars."

Judge Cooper seems to have prided himself on his physical strength and agility. He offered a lot (probably 150 acres of land) as a reward to any man on the settlement who could throw him. The challenge was accepted, the Judge finally thrown by one of the settlers, and the lot conveyed to his conqueror.

William Cooper was appointed First Judge of the Court of Common Pleas of Otsego county in 1791 and held this office until October 1800. His appointment, so the commission reads, was for "such time as he shall well behave himself therein or until he shall attain the age of sixty years." His retirement from office was not due to either limitation. The commission is signed by George Clinton, recited to be "Governor of our said state, General and Commander-in-Chief of all the militia and Admiral of the Navy of the same." He was twice elected to Congress, in 1795 and in 1799, and once lost his election.

The interest in politics during the earlier years of the United States far exceeded that of to-day, and entered largely into the life of all the inhabitants. Nearly every elector seems to have been a politician. The letters of the time are full of politics and party animosity. Judge Cooper, a federalist, was a prominent member of his party and devoted much of his time to its cause. He was on intimate terms with its leaders, and in constant correspondence with many of them.

The population in the country was scanty, and as the franchise was restricted by a property qualification, the voters were comparatively few; but the enthusiasm was unlimited. The polls could be kept open five days, so as to accomodate all wanting to vote, and as there was no secret ballot the excitement was constant and intense. Jacob Morris, writing of an election in Unadilla (Otsego county) at which 141 votes were cast, and the federalist majority was five, after dwelling on the completeness of the victory, says: "Our success is wholly ascribable to the federal spirit of the Butternuts; the hardy sons of this new settlement, rushed over the Otego hills, an irresistible phalanx"—and then referring to his political opponents, adds:

"That since in political dust they are laid
They're all dead and d———d and no more can be said."

There are frequent complaints in the letters of fraud and of the influence and prominence of foreigners, especially the Irish. Fear for the future of the country and the stability of property is expressed in almost the terms used to-day. The federalists are "friends of order" and their opponents "anti-Christians", "enemies of the country" etc. One prominent resident of Otsego county and of Philadelphia, writes: "We are busy about electing a senator in the state legislature. The contest is between B. R. M—, a gentleman, and consequently a federalist, and a dirty stinking anti-federal Jew tavern-keeper called I. I—. But, Judge, the friends to order here don't understand the business, they are uniformly beaten, we used to order these things better at Cooperstown."

Philip Schuyler, writing to Judge Cooper of the election of 1791, says: "I believe fasting and prayer to be good, but if you had only fasted and prayed I am sure we should not have had seven hundred votes from your country—report says that you was very civil to the young and handsome of the sex, that you flattered the old and ugly, and even embraced the toothless and decrepid, in order to obtain votes. When will you write a treatise on electioneering? Whenever you do, afford only a few copies to your friends."

Campaigns were not, however, always conducted on such peaceful and pleasant lines, as appears from the following affidavits, a number of printed copies of which are among Judge Cooper's papers, endorsed in his handwriting, "Oath how I whipped Cochran." They were apparently used as campaign documents. The James Cochran referred to was a political opponent, and defeated Cooper for Congress at an earlier date.

"Jessie Hyde, of the town of Warren, being duly sworn, saith, that on the sixteenth day of October in the year 1799, he this deponent, did see James Cochran make an assault upon William Cooper in the public highway. That the said William Cooper defended himself, and in the struggle Mr. Cochran, in a submissive manner, requested of Judge Cooper to let him go.

JESSIE HYDE.

Sworn this sixteenth day of }
October, 1799, before me, }
Richard Edwards, Master in Chancery."

"OTSEGO COUNTY, ss.

Personally appeared Stephen Ingalls, one of the constables of the town of Otsego, and being duly sworn, deposeth and saith, that he was present at the close of a bruising match between James Cochran, Esq. and William Cooper, Esq. on or about the sixteenth of October last, when the said James Cochran confessed to the said William Cooper these words: "I acknowledge you are too much of a buffer for me," at which time it was understood, as this deponent conceives, that Cochran was confessedly beaten.

STEPHEN INGALS.

Sworn before me this sixth day }
of November, 1799. }
Joshua Dewey, Justice of the Peace."

In the election of 1792 the state canvassers, acting upon the advice of Aaron Burr, rejected, for alleged irregularity in the manner of their return, certain votes and among them those of Otsego county, and by so doing changed the result of the election, defeated Jay, and declared Clinton elected governor. This action caused great indignation among the federalists and seems to have been unjustified. As a means of diverting attention from it, a petition, charging Judge Cooper with having unduly influenced the voters in his county, was presented to the state legislature. An investigation was had, and the petition finally dismissed as frivolous and vexatious. Judging from the personal letters on the subject written Cooper at the time, the charges were groundless.

Judge Cooper died at Albany, December 22, 1809, as the result of a blow on the head, struck from behind, by an opponent as they were leaving a political meeting.

This "Guide in the Wilderness" was not published until after his death, and it gives an excellent idea of the man. The letters composing it show Judge Cooper to have been a close observer of nature, a man who saw and understood the value of the natural phenomena among which he lived, and a student of character. That he was of a kindly disposition the letters which exist among his papers show. He made some bitter enemies, as was inevitable with a man leading so active a life and taking so great an interest in politics as he, but he had many devoted friends.

William Sampson, to whom the letters composing "The Guide in the Wilderness" were written, was a well-known lawyer. He was born in Londonderry in 1764 and died in New York in 1836. He was the son of a Presbyterian minister, and an officer of the Irish Volunteers. He was counsel at Dublin for members of the Society of United Irishmen. After the failure of the revolution in 1798, he fled from Ireland but was brought back to Dublin and eventually allowed his freedom upon the condition of his living in Portugal, where he was afterwards imprisoned at the instance of the English government, but was finally set at liberty and came to this country. He wrote a number of books, among them his own memoirs, of which three editions were published.

The following extract from a letter of his to Judge Cooper explains the reason for the publication of the "Guide" in Dublin and fixes the date of the letters as prior to 1807.

Sir:— Since you left us I have been too much occupied with moving, attendance on the courts, and other matters to have made much progress respecting our little work. I have however employed my spare moments towards making a fair transcript of your letters. The booksellers here give little encouragement, or to say better, very great discouragement to any literary object, and unless they have it for nothing to themselves they seem to make it a point to keep it down. But there is a ship about to sail shortly for Belfast or Londonderry, in both of which quarters I have brothers, men of liberal minds and passionate for useful knowledge. I have no doubt your letters will interest them highly, and the public no less. And although neither your object in writing those letters nor mine in publishing them was to get money, yet I should think that going to the expense of printing a work so likely to be productive to a publisher would be useless. I wish to have your consent before I take any further step, and shall be glad to hear how your health has been and what there is new in your woods . . . .   I am sir,

Your friend and humble servant,
WILLIAM SAMPSON.
"New York, 12th of May, 1807."

In this republication, the original text has been strictly followed, and there appear all of the mistakes in spelling and grammatical errors existing in the pamphlet as first published—for some of them the author is probably responsible, for others the printer.

JAMES FENIMORE COOPER.

Albany, March, 1897.

A GUIDE IN THE WILDERNESS

LETTER FROM WILLIAM SAMPSON, ESQ., TO JUDGE COOPER.

Sir:— Our late conversations have awakened in me the strongest desire to be better informed on a subject so interesting. It seems generally allowed that you are peculiarly qualified to give a faithful and useful account of the cultivation of the American woods. Whatever our respective opinions may be as to the advantage of foreign commerce, in this we both agree, that the first and best of arts is agriculture; it is in my opinion most conducive to the welfare of this new country, most congenial to its mild policy and happy institutions, and doubly deserving of attention when the violence of foreign powers threatens the existence of commerce, and seems imperiously to dictate a recurrence to internal resources.

Many crude and conceited things have been given to the world by running writers and traveling book-makers; but so far from being of any authority, they have rendered it still more necessary to seek information at some authenic source.

Those whose object is, at all events to write, are apt to take the subject by the wrong end.

They first form a theory, and then go about collecting facts to prove it. These are not much to be relied on. But he who has acquired by long practice and repeated experience a knowledge of many facts, can scarcely err in theory. His theory will be no more than that generalization which is the instinctive process of every intelligent mind; it will be impossible for him to wander into fanciful errors, for the number of facts of which he has the certainty will come in aid of his judgment, and rise in the defense of truth.

I consider besides, that the success of your plans gives great weight to your authority. For though I would not condemn measures merely because they fail, yet it is a good proof of their fitness that they succeed. And who would not prefer as a guide, the man that found his way, to him that lost himself.

Your knowledge has been all practical, all profitable; the face of immense tracts of country bears testimony of this, and thousands of living witnesses confirm it. It would be, therefore, a subject of regret, if you should be disposed to withhold that knowledge from others, which has been so useful to yourself.

And I should hope that the communication would be attended with some pleasure, and that the liberal and manly enterprise of reclaiming from its rude state the barren wilderness, and scattering the smiling habitations of civilized man in those dreary wastes, when for nought appearing, the wandering savage had not before imprinted the image of his foot, must be dear to the recollection of him whose courage and perseverance has triumphed over so many difficulties.

If success in such enterprises be not glory, it is something better; and in any rational view it is doubtless preferable to the distinctions earned by political craft, or won in the lawless career of war. Leave to Caesar the boast of having destroyed two millions of men; let yours be that of having cut down two millions of trees. He made men disappear from the fruitful soil where they were born; your labors made a new and happier race appear where none before had been. To say that you have done all this for your own interest, does not take away the merit; but to render your labors useful to others, and lend the lights of experience to those who may stand in need of them, is the duty to which I now invite you. Good rules of practice are essential to the farmer and to the landholder. Minute details of experiment are precious to the philosopher, although made with no view to his utility, and the honest statesman will never disdain to learn by what means the resources of his country can be best improved.

But there is another class for whom I feel a warmer interest; the poor, the unfortunate, whom want and oppression drive from their native land, to seek an asylum beyond the waves of the ocean, where inexhaustible regions lie open to their industry; where peace and toleration invite them to take refuge and the genius of equal law and liberty beckons them to security and consolation.

Thus it is in your power to befriend the wealthy capi-

talist and the poor emigrant, and at the same time to
give agreeable instruction to such whose liberal range of
thought carries them beyond the little sphere of self, and
who will be pleased to see by what means the face of
nature can be altered, and how in half the span of one
man's life, towns, roads and cheerful seats, with all the
comforts of civilized life, can be substituted for the gloomy
monotony of the barren desert.

You may perhaps say that what I ask would be a history of your own life, and I confess as far as discretion
will permit, I should desire to know that part of it which
is interwoven with the subject. I should delight to follow
your first steps through the Wilderness; to conceive all
the difficulties you had to surmount, and the means by
which you overcame them. I should then have instruction
conveyed in the most interesting manner, with all the
advantages of example, precept, and proof. I am, sir,
with respect and friendship,

Your obedient Servant,
WILLIAM SAMPSON.

QUERIES.

I. Which is the best way for the purchaser of a large
tract of forest or unsettled lands to bring it into a productive state? What profit he ought reasonably to expect
whilst he leaves to the tenant or settler the means of
advancing himself? In short, what is the interest, and
what the duty of such landlord?

II. What description of men is best qualified and most
likely to settle in the Wilderness and become farmers?
How they should proceed? Are mechanics apt to prosper?

III. What part of the state is best situated for present
or future market? Where are the principal places of
deposit for the produce of each part? How far natural
or artificial means may open others, and when it is probable that great leading roads will be made or encouraged
by the state? How far canals would be advantageous,
productive, and practicable?

IV. Is there much variety in the soil? If so, what is

best for each several kind of culture? How far is the soil
and climate favorable to the growth of fruit trees, vegetables, grain, grass, flax, hemp, &c.? To what use can the
trees of the forest be best turned? Is the timber durable
for fencing, building, &c.? Is there no reason to fear
that too great zeal for clearing may render it in some
time as scarce as it is now abundant?

V. What domestic animals are most profitable to the
farmer? What are the wild beasts of the forest? What
are useful or noxious to the settler? Are there fish? Of
what kinds? How plenty? Is there much game? Are
there valuable furs? How are they obtained?

VI. By what indications may the quality of the soil be
known?

VII. What progress have manufacturers made in the
new settlements? What are the raw materials? What
the encouragement? What are the principal exports?

In answering these Queries I should request you not
to confine yourself to the heads therein specified. My
ignorance of the subject—it being one upon which I have
never meditated—makes it impossible for me to point to
all its details, and therefore it is that the history of your
own progress in the various settlements you have made,
would be the best answer possible to the whole of my
questions. How far you suffered from inexperience in
the first undertakings, where you have erred or failed, or
have observed others to do so from the same cause; what
motives first led you to adventure in the Wilderness,
example, necessity, or taste?

LETTER FROM JUDGE COOPER TO WILLIAM
SAMPSON, ESQ.

Sir:— I shall cheerfully answer the Queries you have
put to me. The manly way in which you have challenged
me, and the good sense you have shown upon a subject of
which you can have no experience, and the object I pre-
ceive you have at heart, that of procuring information in
a matter interesting to your countrymen, does you honor,

and makes it a pleasure for me to satisfy so fair a curiosity. I shall answer each query in the order you have proposed them; and, although that knowledge acquired by practice alone cannot well be imparted, yet I feel, I believe, the bent of your inquiries, and shall do all in my power to make my answers useful, as well to your countrymen as to my own.

I shall first make the general supposition, that either a wealthy individual or else a company purchase a large tract of land, say 50,000 acres. The purchaser, or some one strongly interested in the purchase, should go upon the spot, and give public notice of the day when he means to open the sales. The conditions should be advertised, and notice given, that every person desirous of buying should have as much or as little as he chose, on a credit of seven or ten years, paying annual interest. The price will naturally vary according to soil and situation.

It should be distinctly understood that the whole tract is open for settlement without any reserve on the part of the landlord, as nothing is more discouraging than any appearance in him of views distinct from the prosperity of the whole; and this would be evident if in the very outset he reserved any part in contemplation of a future advance, at the expense of the labor of the original settlers, to whose advantage these reserved tracts had not contributed. The reason is plain; the first difficulties are the greatest, and it is only by combination and coöperation that they can be surmounted. The more the settlers are in number, the more hands can be brought to affect those works which cannot be executed by a few; such are the making of roads and bridges, and other incidents to the cultivation of the Wilderness, which are impossible to individuals, but which numbers render practicable and easy.

Besides, he who comes to better his condition, by embarking in such an enterprise would find it no relief from his present poverty, to be doomed to a life of savage solitude; he will still desire the society of his species, and the ordinary comforts of life; he will look for some religious institution, some school for his children. There must be mechanics to build houses, and erect mills, and other useful or necessary purposes. Where there are a number of settlers, each bearing his proportion of the labor, and contributing to the expense, these things arise almost of course, but it would be very discouraging to a few scattered settlers to reflect that they were toiling under all the hardships and disadvantages of a new and arduous undertaking, whilst others, who had contributed nothing, should afterwards come in and reap all the advantages of their activity. The reserved tracts, therefore, serving only to separate from each other, and depriving them of the comforts of society, and of the advantage of coöperation, would be sources of just discontent, and the landlord who seemed to harbor the ungenerous project of trafficing with the future profits of their industry, and to give all his care to his own interest, without any sympathy with them, would become deservedly an object of distrust and jealousy; his influence would cease, and that confidence, which could alone animate and invigorate a difficult enterprise, once vanishing, nothing but failure could ensue.

Thus the advantage of the landlord is to reserve no part, if he can possibly dispose of it. Sometimes a man of large property with an enterprising spirit, will seek for a tract suitable to his means and his ambition. Such a one may have friends and connections, who may want courage to face the first difficulties, or venture on untried ways, but whom he hopes to draw after him by example. It is of great importance to promote the success of such a person, and he will be justly entitled to kindness and support. His task will be to smooth the way for others. As soon as he is himself seated, his next wish will be to draw around him a neighborhood of relatives and friends, whose habits are congenial to his own. He will be repaid for his labor and risk by selling at a small advance beyond the price he paid, and the interest upon it. Such, besides that he will come provided with stock and capital, will be useful, as it were, to sound the horn and proclaim the settlement, and will be a new centre of attraction.

But, while we acknowledge the importance of the wealthy undertaker, we must not despise the offer of the poor man. He can never be insignificant who is willing to add his labor to the common stock, for the interest of every individual from the richest landholder to the poorest settler conspires and contributes to the great primary object, to cause the Wilderness to bloom and fructify; and each man prospers in proportion as he contributes to the advantage of his neighbor.

With respect to the lands: although they will naturally vary in quality, I never in the first existance make any difference in price, but leave that matter to regulate itself. In the beginning the poorer settler will refuse the rougher spots, and rightly, as they will yield him no immediate subsistence. I therefore leave them until that period when the timber they afford shall become valuable for the purpose of fencing and for fuel; and by the simple measure of letting things take their own course, I find my interest and that of the whole community promoted; and in no instance have the rough grounds and the swamps failed to be eventually most profitable to me; nay, in fifteen years' time their value has increased to seven fold.

The poor man, and his class is the most numerous, will generally undertake about one hundred acres. The best mode of dealing with him is to grant him the fee-simple by deed, and secure the purchase money by a mortgage on the land conveyed to him. He then feels himself, if I may use the phrase, as a man upon record. His views extend themselves to his posterity, and he contemplates with pleasure their settlement on the estate he has created; a sentiment ever grateful to the heart of man, his spirit is enlivened, his industry is quickened, every new object he attains brings a new ray of hope and courage; he builds himself a barn and a better habitation, plants his fruit trees, and lays out his garden; he clears away the trees, until they, which were the first obstacles to his improvement, becoming scarcer, become more valuable, and he is at length as anxious to preserve as he was at first to destroy them; he no longer feels the weight of debt, for having the fee he can sell at an improved value, nor is he bound to remain against his will.

Not so if he had been bound by special contracts and conditions, subjecting him to the forfeiture of his land, and with it of his labor. Gloomy apprehensions then seize upon his mind, the bright view of independence is clouded, his habits of thought become sullen and cheerless, and he is unable to soar above the idea of perpetual poverty.

Thus, by the adoption of a rational plan, it appears that the interest of all parties are made to coincide. The settler sleeps in security, from the certainty of his possession, and the landlord is safe in the mortgage he holds, and the state profits by the success of each, in the increase of its wealth and population.

A moderate price, long credit, a deed in fee, and a friendly landlord are infallible inducements to a numerous settlement, and where there is much people there will be trade; and where there is trade there will be money; and where there is money the landlord will succeed; but he should be ever in the midst of the settlers, aiding and promoting every beneficial enterprise.

In this point of view I have often compared the dealer in land to a ship. Money is the element he swims in; without money he is aground; and as a ship that is not afloat is no better than a wreck, so when he ceases to have money his activity and usefulness are gone.

So, in rural phrase, may we compare the poor settler to the creature of draft. Unsustained, over-loaded, and oppressed, he yields no profit; well treated in good heart, and gently driven, his labor is lighter and his profit more. It is not otherwise with man. He can bear so much and no more; if forced beyond that his spirits will finally sink under oppression; whereas, by timely aids, encouraging words from a landlord, who has his confidence, and whom he feels to be his friend, he will perform wonders and exceed his own hopes.

You have desired to know something of my own proceedings, and since I am to speak of myself, I can nowhere better introduce that subject than now, in proof of what I have asserted.

I began with the disadvantage of a small capital, and the encumbrance of a large family, and yet I have already settled more acres than any man in America. There are forty thousand souls now holding, directly or indirectly, under me, and I trust that no one amongst so many can justly impute to me any act resembling oppression. I am now descending into the vale of life, and I must acknowledge that I look back with self complacency upon what I have done, and am proud of having been an instrument in reclaiming such large and fruitful tracts from the waste of the creation. And I question whether that sensation is not now a recompense more grateful to me than all the other profits I have reaped. Your good sense and knowledge of the world will excuse this seeming boast; if it be vain (we all must have our vanities), let it at least serve to show that industry has its reward, and age its pleasures, and be an encouragement to others to persevere and prosper.

In 1785 I visited the rough and hilly country of Otsego, where there existed not an inhabitant, nor any trace of a road; I was alone, three hundred miles from home, without bread, meat, or food of any kind; fire and fishing tackle were my only means of subsistence. I caught trout in the brook and roasted them on the ashes. My horse fed on the grass that grew by the edge of the waters. I laid me down to sleep in my watch coat, nothing but the melancholy Wilderness around me. In this way I explored the country, formed my plans of future settlement, and meditated upon the spot where a place of trade or a village should afterwards be established.

In May, 1786, I opened the sales of 40,000 acres, which in sixteen days were all taken up by the poorest order of men. I soon after established a store, and went to live among them, and continued so to do till 1790, when I brought on my family. For the ensuing four years the scarcity of provisions was a serious calamity; the country was mountainous, and there were neither roads nor bridges.

But the greatest discouragement was in the extreme poverty of the people, none of whom had the means of clearing more than a small spot in the midst of the thick and lofty woods, so that their grain grew chiefly in the shade; their maize did not ripen, their wheat was blasted, and the little they did gather they had no mill to grind within twenty miles distance; not one in twenty had a horse, and the way lay through rapid streams, across swamps or over bogs. They had neither provisions to take with them nor money to purchase them; nor if they had, were any to be found on their way. If the father of a family went abroad to labor for bread, it cost him three times its value before he could bring it home, and all the business on his farm stood still till his return.

I resided among them, and saw too clearly how bad their condition was. I erected a store-house, and during each winter filled it with large quantities of grain, purchased in distant places. I procured from my friend Henry Drinker a credit for a large quantity of sugar kettles; he also lent me some potash kettles, which we conveyed as we best could, sometimes by partial roads on sleighs, and sometimes over the ice. By this means I established potash works among the settlers, and made them debtor for their bread and laboring utensils. I also gave them credit for their maple sugar and potash, at a price that would bear transportation, and the first year after the adoption of this plan I collected in one mass forty-three hogsheads of sugar, and three hundred barrels of pot and pearl ash, worth about nine thousand dollars. This kept the people together and at home, and the country soon assumed a new face.

I had not funds of my own sufficient for the opening of new roads, but I collected the people at convenient seasons, and by joint efforts we were able to throw bridges over the deep streams, and to make, in the cheapest manner, such roads as suited our then humble purposes.

In the winter preceding the summer of 1789, grain rose in Albany to a price before unknown. The demand swept all the granaries of the Mohawk country. The number of beginners who depended upon it for their bread, greatly aggravated the evil, and a famine ensued which will never be forgotten by those who, though now in the enjoyment of ease and comfort, were then afflicted with the cruelest of wants.

In the month of April I arrived amongst them with several loads of provisions, destined for my own use and that of the laborers I had brought with me for certain necessary operations; but in a few days all was gone, and there remained not one pound of salt meat, nor a single biscuit. Many were reduced to such distress as to live upon the root of wild leeks; some more fortunate lived upon milk, whilst others supported nature by drinking a syrup made of maple sugar and water. The quantity of leeks they eat had such an effect upon their breath that they could be smelled at many paces distant, and when they came together it was like cattle that had been pastured in a garlic field. A man of the name of Beets mistaking some poisonous herb for a leek, eat it, and died in consequence. Judge of my feelings at this epoch, with two hundred families about me and not a morsel of bread.

A singular event seemed sent by a good Providence to our relief; it was reported to me that unusual shoals of fish were seen moving in the clear waters of the Susquehanna. I went, and was surprised to find that they were herrings. We made something like a small net, by the interweaving of twigs, and by this rude and simple contrivance we were able to take them in thousands. In less than ten days each family had an ample supply with plenty of salt. I also obtained from the Legislature, then in session, seventeen hundred bushels of corn. This we packed on horses' backs, and on our arrival made a distribution among the families, in proportion to the number of individuals of which each was composed.

This was the first settlement I made, and the first attempted after the Revolution; it was, of course, attended with the greatest difficulties; nevertheless, to its success many others have owed their origin. It was besides the roughest land in all the state, and the most difficult of cultivation of all that had been settled; but for many years past it has produced everything necessary to the support and comfort of man. It maintains at present eight thousand souls, with schools, academies, churches, meeting-houses, turnpike roads, and a market town. It annually yields to commerce large droves of fine oxen, great quantities of wheat and other grain, abundance of pork, potash in barrels, and other provisions; merchants with large capitals, and all kinds of useful mechanics reside upon it; the waters are stocked with fish, the air is salubrious, and the country thriving and happy. When I contemplate all this, and above all, when I see these good old settlers meet together, and hear them talk of past hardships, of which I bore my share, and compare the misery they then endured with the comforts they now enjoy, my emotions border upon weakness which manhood can scarcely avow. One observation more on the duty of landlords shall close my answer to your first inquiry.

If the poor man who comes to purchase land has a cow and a yoke of cattle to bring with him, he is of the most fortunate class, but as he will probably have no money to hire a laborer, he must do all his clearing with his own hands. Having no pasture for his cow and oxen, they must range the woods for subsistence; he must find his cow before he can have his breakfast, and his oxen before he can begin his work. Much of the day is sometimes wasted, and his strength uselessly exhausted.. Under all these disadvantages, if in three years he attains a comfortable livelihood, he is pretty well off; he will then require a barn, as great losses accrue from the want of shelter for his cattle and his grain; his children, yet too young to afford him any aid, require a school, and are a burden upon him; his wife bearing children, and living poorly in an open house is liable to sickness, and doctors' bills will be to pay. If then, in addition to all this, he should be pressed by his landlord, he sinks under his distress; but if, at this critical moment, he be assisted and encouraged, he will soon begin to rise. The landlord should first give him a fair time; if after that he cannot pay the principal money, he may take from him a release of the equity of redemption, and then grant him a lease forever with a clause of fee on payment of the principal, and the rent reserved, which it would be well to make payable in wheat, with a moderate advance on the first price and interest.

Indeed, justice and policy combine to point out the duty of the landlord; for if a man has struggled ten years in vain, and is at the end of that time unable to pay, not only humanity, but self-interest dictates another course, and some new expedient for reciprocal advantage. So here, the tenant instead of being driven for the principal, will not only keep his possession, but retain the privilege of re-acquiring the principal at a future day, by the very produce of the lands. He will be happy in the idea of still preserving his home, will pay his rent with cheerfulness, and the landlord has so much certainly added to his capital, whether the tenant repurchases the fee or not; the improvements if he does purchase it, and if not, the price agreed upon.

Therefore, independently of the reasons above given, it is better for the landlord to accept of the poorest settler than to reserve tracts in his own hands, because every part of the land by this means is made to contribute to the common stock of labor, coöperation, and general improvement, and because he has a better profit by the consent of the individual, and consistent with the advantage of all.

For example: if you sell one hundred acres for one hundred pounds, with interest at the end of ten years, it will amount to one hundred and seventy pounds; and though the tenant cannot presently pay this sum (at least without selling his farm), yet the landlord has his security for it in his mortgage-deed, and the improved value of the land, and is therefore no loser by the delay. In most instances the tenant will be very unwilling to sell the farm he has re-claimed with so much pains, and, worn with years and labor, to enter upon the hardships of a new undertaking. He sees that his land is now in good order and productive, and that he will be able easily to pay the yearly rent of fourteen pounds in produce, and that he can always acquire the disposal of the fee simple upon performance of the condition.

Having now given you an idea of the difficulties of our first settlement, it is right I should observe to you that the settlement of lands in general is not at this day attended with such obstacles. In many parts of the state the soil is so fine, and so many settlements are already formed throughout, that the rest will follow of course; but still the landlord who resides on the spot, and pursues such track as I have pointed out, will succeed with much the most certainty, and will gain many years of time.

Some rich theorists let the property they purchase lie unoccupied and unproductive, and speculate upon a full indemnity from the future rise in value, the more so as they feel no want of the immediate profits. But I can assert from practical experience that it is better for a poor man to pay forty shillings an acre to a landlord who heads the settlement, and draws people around him by good

plans for their advancement, and arrangements for
their convenience, than to receive an hundred acres gratis
from one of these wealthy theorists; for if fifty thousand
acres be settled, so that there is but one man upon a
thousand acres, there can be no one convenience of life
attainable; neither roads, school, church, meeting, nor any
other of those advantages, without which man's life would
resemble that of a wild beast.

Of this I had full proof in the circumstances of the
Burlington Company; they were rich and purchased a
tract of sixty-nine thousand acres, and made a deed of
gift of one hundred acres out of each thousand to actual
settlers, and this they were bound to do in compliance with
the condition in the King's patent. They provided these
settlers with many articles of husbandry under the particular agency of Mr. Nathaniel Edwards. But he very
soon returned, and not long afterward the settlers followed, stating that they could not support themselves so
far in the woods in that scattered situation.

I then resided in Burlington, and when I undertook to
make the settlement on those very lands where so rich a
company had failed, it was thought a romantic undertaking
for a man unprovided with funds to attempt what gra-
tuitous donations had not been able to achieve. Nevertheless I succeeded, and for that very reason that I made
no partial gifts, but sold the whole at a moderate price
with easy payments, having for myself a handsome profit;
and people were readily induced to come when they saw
a number of coöperators, and the benefits of association.

You have now before you, as well as I can explain, the
advantages and the difficulties which belong to an enterprise in new lands. But let me be clearly understood in
this, that no man who does not possess a steady mind, a
sober judgment, fortitude, perseverance, and above all,
common sense, can expect to reap the reward which to him
who possesses those qualifications is almost certain.

W. C.

That part of the State of New York which includes
the counties of Oneida, Onondaga, Cayuga, Madison,
Otsego, Steuben, Lewis, Jefferson, Clinton, Broome, and

Essex, are the tracts that have been settled since 1786, and certainly contain more fine lands than are to be found contiguous in any part of the United States. They extend from the forty-second to the forty-fifth degree of latitude, and from the eastern to the western extremity upwards of two hundred miles. This region is everywhere intersected by rivers, navigable in small boats of about three tons burden, by means of which the produce of every part may be transported to tide-water and a sea-port.

The counties of Tioga, Otsego, Broome, Chenango, Steuben, and Allegany, have the Susquehanna and its branches; for instance, the Tioga with its branches carries off the produce of Allegany and Steuben counties. Upon the Chenango they float the produce of Madison and Chenango, with abundance of salt to different places in the Susquehanna, and their wheat and lumber to Baltimore. Of the outlet by the Mohawk I shall speak hereafter.

The Unadilla passes between the counties of Chenango and Otsego, and is navigable in the spring for boats, rafts, and arks; perhaps this latter term may to you require an explanation. An ark then, is neither strictly a boat nor a raft, but partakes of the nature of each; it is of the form of a lozenge, so that each angle operates as a wedge; this figure is found convenient, as it admits more rapidly of a lateral deflection, and in case of sudden interruption in its course by shoals or other obstacles. It is hastily and cheaply constructed, and is not even water tight, but the bottom is fitted up with light timber, so that it is buoyant enough to keep the grain and other perishable produce from being wet.

In these arks a surprising quantity of wheat is annually conveyed to Baltimore, besides much that finds a market far short of that port, at Harrisburg, Middleburg, and Columbia, three considerable trading towns on this river within the state of Pennsylvania, and had not this latter state lost somewhat of its ancient spirit of enterprise, the whole of this trade might have centered in it; for the navigation which is free from all obstruction as far as Columbia, is interrupted before it reaches Maryland by the Bald-Friar and Turkey river falls, both of which are dangerous and difficult to descend, and impracticable in their ascent.

The Seneca Lake is forty miles long, and out of it boats can pass as far as Schenectady, which is within fourteen miles of the tide water of the Hudson. At this place their loading must be landed, on account of the interruption to the navigation by the Cohoes falls lower down on the Mohawk near the town of Waterford; by this means the produce of Ontario County is brought to market.

The Cayuga lake is about the same length, and has a good passage for boats with the produce of Seneca, Cayuga, and part of Tioga counties.

From the Onondaga or Salt Lake, besides the produce of the adjacent lands, great quantities of salt are sent in every direction. With a small land carriage they arrive at the salt landing in the town of Homer, on the navigable waters of the Chenango river, and from this point a great scope of country is supplied with that precious article. Boats carrying from forty to fifty tons have water sufficient for the transport of such a cargo into the neighboring lakes; the county of Upper Canada, the shores of lakes Erie, Huron, Michigan, and Superior, with the shores of the Saint Lawrence and the many navigable rivers leading into it, can be thus furnished at a cheap rate with a never failing supply. In short, it seems as if nature had exhausted her favors within the boundaries I am treating of.

The counties of Oneida and Lewis have the convenience of Utica and Rome upon the Mohawk. The county of Genesee has the two great lakes, Ontario and Erie, on its margin, from whence there is an issue in every direction. The county of Jefferson has the lake Ontario and several fine harbors. The county of Saint Lawrence has that magnificent river from which it takes its name; the Oswegatchie, which falls into the Saint Lawrence after a navigable course of seventy miles; the Richet and Saint Regis which cut the country into convenient sections for trade, and this is, in my judgment, toil and trade considered, a county as valuable as any in the state.

Clinton and Essex counties have lake Champlain with all its inlets and outlets.

As to those places likely to become principal emporia or great markets, there are many of them. I shall point out some which cannot possibly fail to become important, unless crippled by the contracted views of those who may be proprietors of the soil.

I have already shown the impolicy of reserving certain tracts in a new settlement on the speculation of their future rise in value. This mistake, where trade is the object, is still more pernicious, for as liberty is in my apprehension the very child of commerce, so the one will not remain where the other cannot be. To make commerce thrive you must make it free, and where there is not freedom there will not be trade, and all useless restrictions and reservations are more or less clogging to the active disposition of property, and to the freedom of men's choice and will.

The proprietor of a spot favorable for commerce should refuse no part of it to a good mechanic or trader. He should reserve no spot when such a tenant offers. He should not aim at partial advantages, but look to the more liberal profits which are to arise out of the stock of general prosperity; and in all cases he should grant the fee, without which the tenant will never improve with spirit, nor build himself a good house. If the proprietor stands in his own light, and takes the opposite course, he will have the mortification to find some neighboring spot, with fewer natural advantages outstrip him in prosperity, and cast him entirely in the shade.

And I hold it essential to the progress of a trading town, that it be settled quickly and compactly, and the only point in which I would thwart the wishes of the settler, whether merchant or mechanic, would be in the desire which most entertain of possessing a large lot. It is for his own advantage that this should be resisted, for if he be half tradesman and half farmer he will neither prosper as one nor as the other. There should be a mutual dependence between the farmer and the villager; the farmer relying upon the villager for the purchase of his produce, and the villager upon the farmer for the sale of the articles of his trade. If the mechanic will have a farm, or even a large garden or orchard, or if he devotes his time in any manner to the cultivation of the ground, even to the raising what is sufficient for his own consumption, it is impossible he should be so active and vigilant in his profession as he would otherwise be; for instance, the barber, instead of being in the way to shave his customers, will be found weeding his onions; the shoemaker hoeing his potatos; the watchmaker, who has neglected to repair the farmer's watch, will think it an excuse that his orchard required his immediate care; the blacksmith, who has been tilling the ground, when he should have been providing himself with coal, will be unable to shoe the traveler's horse, or mend the carrier's wagon. It is not he alone then that remains idle, but if it could be calculated how much the loss of time and of the opportunities of profit is multiplied by each of these delays, it would be the most solid of all arguments. He, perhaps, who waits for the barber to shave him, has been charged by his neighbors with various commissions, and their business, like his own, must stand still till he returns; obliged to loiter, he goes, perhaps, to the tavern, spends his money, wastes his time, and gets drunk. Want of punctuality in one man occasions the same in others, and dilatory habits are the consequence, and it will be found that no industry in his outdoor labor can pay the mechanic for the loss of diligence within. The traveler, again, is from the negligence of the smith forced to proceed with his horse unshod, his beast becomes lame, he is delayed, perhaps benighted, and obliged to waste his time and money at an inn; the wagoner who cannot have his wheel repaired, is obliged to wait, and his team stand idle; the farmer has no watch to regulate his time, and wastes much of it in repeated calls for it. These frivolous disappointments familiarize the mind to irregularity and procrastination, the most pernicious of all habits in an early settlement; and if there be another village or another market, though more inconvenient or more distant, where every man is to be found at his post, the mechanic in his workshop, the merchant in his store, such a place will carry off the prize of industry, and become the rendezvous of traffic and prosperity.

The case will be quite different where the people are settled on small lots without either garden or orchard.

They will there be all found in their shops or workhouses, and in that manner the diligent and steady man never fails to gain a good and certain livlihood. The farmer will choose a town so circumstanced as a market for his produce, and will generally receive in payment from the trader, goods to the full amount, and often become his debtor for more to be paid at his next visit; and this credit operates as an increase of capital, and promotes the activity of all.

On the other hand, villages and trading towns built on extensive lots, where the inhabitants are dispersed, never make much progress in trade. They have all the disadvantages of towns, without their comforts and convenience. A thousand little clashings of interest, and sources of altercations arise between neighbors; the poultry of the one destroy the garden of the other, or the pigs commit trespasses; and such trifling accidents repeated and resented, engender disputes and enmities.

One argument for building in this detached manner is the danger of fire, where wooden houses, as these must be, are crowded together and contiguous; but when it is considered that help is more remote, the sense of common danger less pressing, and therefor the energy in surmounting the evil less excited, the argument may be turned the other way.

Certainly when the inhabitants are at a distance from each other there is less society, less useful communication upon subjects of common concern, such as the eduation of children and the like; there is less polish of manners, more carelessness in dress and demeanor, and more languor and indifference in every sort of improvement. But in towns compactly built there is a quicker circulation of sentiment, and mutual convenience; each follows his own art without deviation, and becomes more perfect in it; there is more emulation; a kind of city pride arises, and acts advantageously upon the manners and modes of life; better houses are built, more comforts introduced, and there is more civility and civilization.

Where one family can support itself by trade upon one acre, sixteen families upon the same acre, each having a trade, will exist still better. Where one family can earn upon one acre three hundred pounds per annum, sixteen families will earn four thousand eight hundred; and each, though aiming merely at his own private emolument, will be working no less for the common benefit, and they will reciprocally profit by each other's labor.

The labor of two or three hundred industrious men concentrated, is like money collected into a bank; when scattered in distant quarters its effects amount to little; when brought together it resembles the heart, from and to which circulation flows, whilst it gives life and health to the remotest extremes.

A good instance of this is the town of Lancaster in Pennsylvania; without any one natural advantage, nor any that I can perceive, other than that of being in the beginning compactly settled, it has risen to be the seventh in the union in point of population and importance.

It is the same of Cooperstown and of all the others where industry, art, and capital are condensed; and all those originally distributed in large lots have ceased after a few years to increase, insomuch that wherever you will mention a town in which each man has his cow, his team, his wagon, and his barn, you will find it to be a place of little trade, consequently of little wealth; but wherever the artist, the merchant, or man of profession, has neither bread, butter, milk, cheese, flesh meat, nor garden-stuff, but what he purchases with the earnings of his calling, there, I engage, you will find trade, comfort, and plenty; there each living by the art in which he is versed, there will be no awkward waste of time, no slovenly or loitering habits; the baker will live by baking, the butcher by his trade, the flour merchant by buying and by selling; schools, churches, and professional merit will advance; all useful skill will increase. And however strange it has appeared to you that I should, where land is so abundant, propose to restrict the settler in the occupation of it, yet certain it is, that if they would prosper they must choose one of two things: either to have so much land as will employ all their industry and support them by its produce, or to leave its cultivation entirely to others, and betake themselves exclusively to the exercise of their trade.

You seem to be prepossessed with the idea of pleasure

and advantage, in mixing rural labours with the exercise of professions, and of the mechanic arts. Such a picture of human life may gratify the imagination, but it is romantic; and both contentment and wealth lie in the road I have traced, if an extensive field of observation and many years' experience can be trusted.

Having given you my opinion upon the first plan of a trading town, I shall proceed to point out the situations most conspicuously advantageous; these are:

The mouth of Buffalo creek on Lake Erie.

The straits of Niagara below the falls.

The first falls of the Genesee, where there is a fine harbor for ships of two hundred tons.

The greater Sodus on Lake Ontario.

The Oswego falls.

The head navigation of the Black river.

Sackett's harbor on the Ontario lake.

Ogdensburgh, at the mouth of the Oswegatchie.

All of these, if properly managed, must become important places of trade.

In the interior, Rome and Utica are already considerably advanced. The former has the most of natural advantages, but the latter has outstripped it, because more attention has been bestowed upon its interests.

Cooperstown, in point of trade and population, stands next to Utica, and is better built, as the inhabitants have the fee; whereas Utica is all on lease, a circumstance which never fails to depress.

Chenango Point, on the Susquehanna, and Oswego are likely to become considerable places. Canandaigua, and Geneva on Seneca Lake, are already very handsome villages.

The Oxbow in the Oswegatchie, is clearly intended by nature as a point of trade as is also the head of the navigation of the Racket river at the falls of Stockholm.

Many other places of minor importance will present themselves to notice, and wherever capital settles, allied with such natural advantages, it must take root and flourish.

The trade of this vast country must be divided between Montreal and New York, and the half of it be thus lost to the United States, unless an inland communication can be formed from Lake Erie to the Hudson. This project, worthy of a nation's enterprise, has been for some time meditated by individuals. Of its practicability there can be no doubt, whilst the world has as yet produced no work so noble; nor has the universe such another situation to improve. Its obvious utility will hereafter challenge more attention; men of great minds will turn their thoughts and devote their energies to its accomplishment, and I doubt not that it will one day be achieved.

The surface of lake Erie is elevated about 280 feet above the Hudson at Albany. A canal large enough for sloops 50 tons burden, will not only bring the produce of these great and rich tracts of land in the state of New York to its capital, but will secure all the trade and productions of the vast country which surrounds the lakes Erie, Huron, Michigan, and Superior. Were this once effected, a sloop might then perform an inland voyage of seventeen hundred miles!

The trade of lake Erie already supports twenty-three ships, brigs, scows, and sloops, and Ontario twelve. The United States have millions of acres in the Michigan country of which the produce by this operation would be transportable to a market.

How, you ask, and by what funds is this great work to be accomplished? Without presuming that my opinion should be the guide in so important a concern, it is enough if I can point out one way in which it may be possible, and I think the mode I am about to propose not only possible, but very practicable. The State of New York may cede the track of this canal to the United States, and the United States may then grant a charter to a company, with strong rights and immunities, and the fullest security the general laws will admit of against the evils of future wars or civil changes; in short whatever would encourage the European capitalist to adventure in this magnificent enterprise. Let the United States take shares to the amount of ten millions of dollars, which will serve as an encouragement and security to the foreign capitalist, and be a safeguard against the effects of those fluctuations in

councils and public opinions, to which the affairs of men
are every where liable.

The banks of this canal would become a carriage road,
and one of the most beautiful in the universe. That most
attractive and gratifying object of human curiosity, the
falls of Niagara would of itself create a thoroughfare, and
the product of the tolls on the turnpikes and canal gates
would raise a revenue sufficient in a very short time, to
requite the undertakers. No stranger but would make
this tour his object, and no traveler of taste would leave it
uncelebrated. But, as this speculation lies in the province
of fancy and may be treated as a vision, I leave it to its
fate and shall proceed in more direct answer to your
queries touching roads likely to be made or encouraged
by the state; I think they will be the following:

First, from Catskill on the Hudson westward to lake
Erie, through the counties of Delaware, Broome, Steuben,
and Genesee.

Second, from Albany to Niagara.

Third, from Albany through the counties of Saratoga,
and the uncultivated parts of the state, to the county of
St. Lawrence, at or near the long Soo in the St. Lawrence.

Fourth, from Plattsburg on lake Champlain to Rome
or Utica on the Mohawk river.

These ought to be made under the auspices of government, and with these remarks I close my answers and
observations on your third head of inquiries.

SOIL AND CLIMATE

As to soil and climate, there is in the one as in the other a considerable variety; but in all these countries the ground is throughout the winter covered with snow, and whenever there is most snow in winter, there is most grass and most wheat in summer. The snow is emphatically and truly called the poor man's manure. The ground is seldom frozen when the snow is deep, and vegetation is nourished and protected by its covering. The wheat takes a much stronger and deeper root than where the earth is drenched during the winter by heavy rains.

In climates where there is alternate rain and frost, the root perishes; not so with us, although it does sometimes happen that after a warm autumn the wheat will have shot up so far and acquired such a premature exuberance from the strength of the sun that it continues to grow under the snow and is smothered.

Some farmers, to prevent that mischief, will turn their young cattle into it to feed it off, but that is a bad expedient; it is better to sow later, but yet not too late, for that has also its risk and inconvenience, for a cold spring succeeding to a late seed time, will give a light crop. It is a saying amongst old experienced farmers,—"If you get a good crop from late seed, do not tell it to your sons."

In general through the temperate zone the seed ought to be put in the ground from the 10th to the 20th of September; summer wheat, flax, oats, barley, and peas as early as the ground will admit; Indian corn about the 20th of May.

In those countries situated on the great lakes, the snows are lighter, the land less hilly, but the water is not so plenty, nor in general so pure as in the hilly countries; of course they are not so healthy.

Our soil and climate is very favorable to the growth of fruit; the apple grows fair and sound; plums of all kinds large and fair; gooseberries and currants grow wild in the woods, and when cultivated become fine; cherries, pears, and grapes succeed everywhere; peaches, apricots, and nectarines are best in the counties of Ontario, Steuben, Genesee, and Cayuga, but in the hilly counties they are uncertain. It is hoped, however, that in time the air will become tempered to their growth, for the uniform effect of clearing the surface of the soil from the immense timber that overshadows it, is to produce a more moderate temperature of the air. The beams of the sun which till then were absorbed in the thick foliage, act now with their full power upon the bosom of the earth, and produce that glow which necessarily imparts itself to the atmosphere. For instance, when the improvements were rare in the Otsego county, the frost destroyed our fall crops, and no month passed over without frost; but since the surface has been laid open to the sun, we are no longer in fear that our crops will be injured by the autumnal frosts, and for the last two years I have succeeded in peaches of a tolerable quality, although not equal to those which grow further west in the same latitude.

Upon the subject of fruit-trees I have dear-bought experience; for although I have at present an assortment as good as most others, it was not till after repeated failures that I succeeded, nor till after much fruitless trials, and much obstinate perseverance, that I discovered the cause of those failures; it was this; our winters are severe, and if choice or tender fruits are planted in rich ground, or highly manured gardens, and the wood being open and spongy, the frost kills as it would a weed.

Every part of our land is naturally strong enough for plums; the best way of forwarding them is to put about three bushels of clear gravel around the tree when first planted; this keeps the earth moist, lets the water through, and prevents the grass from binding. The tree grows moderately, the wood is firm and hardy, the fruit fair and well flavored, and the tree apt to bear generously.

There are few farms in the seventeen counties I have mentioned that do not show great progress in the cultivation of fruit trees, which are raised in most cases from the seed. Otsego, which was the first settled, now makes a great quantity of cider; and when the trees are duly grafted, produce the best flavored fruits.

The potatoes of those counties are equal to the Irish

potato, and frequently lie in the ground all winter under the snow, without injury from the frost. All other vegetables grow to an uncommon size, and are thought preferable to those raised by gardners near the City of New York.

The mutton of the hilly counties is fat and juicy, and very delicate; the wool fair and the fleece heavy. I have observed generally that the further we go north in the United States, the better we find both beef and mutton; and the further we go south, the smaller and sweeter the pork. Our hogs are apt to grow to a great size, but we cannot make hams equal to those of Virginia and Maryland. Horses grow larger and more robust in the southern states. The air with us is probably too sharp for their growth, therefore the animal is small but hardy.

In those parts where both pasture and hay abound, we give hay to our cattle about the 1st of December, and in April they begin to refuse it. About the same time the farmers in the southern states feed their cattle; but there, if that were neglected their cattle would be of much less growth and stature than ours.

Our bottom grounds produce hemp of an excellent quality, and will, in a few years, produce an ample supply for the United States. Those husbandmen who have made the experiment of its cultivation, have found it very beneficial, and have produced as much as six hundred pounds on an acre.

TIMBER

As to the timber, its utility, its abundance, and its qualities: Wherever this country remains unreclaimed by the labor of the settler, its face is uniformly overshadowed by trees of immense growth; the white pine is the most stately, and it is useful for spars, boards, shingles, rails, and building timber, having the valuable property of resisting for a length of time the action of the weather. A shingle roof of this wood will last fifty years, rails as long, and were it but for these two purposes, a grove of such timber preserved upon a farm will be always valuable.

The sugar-tree, which is found all over these counties, is next in celebrity, and is the best fuel the forest yields, the hickory itself not excepted.

Next in importance are the white, and red, or black oak, the barren oak, found in rocky situations, the piss-oak, so called, because the log when on fire emits water at each end; the butternut, the poplar, the red and white beech, all noble and majestic trees. The elm is in abundance, and the bass wood or linden-tree is found everywhere, but is of little utility, being of a soft texture decaying quickly in the open air. The hickory, besides its excellence as fuel, is of great use for the fabrication of many farming utensils; the cherry, the white, black, and yellow birch, all produce excellent timber for the cabinet makers; the chestnut and hemlock-tree are both useful, but the latter more particularly so, as, like the oak and the beech trees it supplies our tanners with bark.

It is a curious property of the hemlock, that a single stroke of an axe is sufficient to destroy it, from which it has been called the tree of sensibility, or, as the woodman says, the most sensible tree of the forest. It does not immediately perish from the wound, but languishes and never revives. I have myself observed that where a hemlock has been merely marked as a line tree, and only cut through the bark in one spot, at the end of fifteen years it is sure to be found dead. So, when they happen to lie by the road side, and are liable to be fretted and disturbed by cart hubs, they perish in a few years. No ashes are produced from this tree, other than an apparently sandy sediment, except from its bark, which when burned separately produces the very best of ashes.

The pine is the only wood which yields no ashes; the best are those produced from the elm, the bass wood, the sugar-tree, and the beech.

You ask whether there is no danger of a future scarcity of timber? I have always thought there was, and for these reasons: great part of our timber is not only of slow growth but when used for fencing, it is of short duration. Our winters require large supplies of fuel, and we have neither peat nor coal to resort to, when constant consumption in fuel and fencing will have rendered that most necessary article scarce. Nor have we other mountainous lands to resort to for wood, nor stony ground for the construction of stone fences. The soil being all fit for culture, will be all cultivated, and the wood of course wasted.

WILD BEASTS

The principal wild beasts of our forests are, the bear, the black and grey wolf and the panther. These are all called noxious animals and so considered by our laws, which give rewards for their destruction, which in these new countries are sometimes as high as from ten to twenty-five dollars, paid on the production of each pair of ears and scalp. Some of the settlers have great address in contriving traps for them, and a poor man sometimes renders himself of good service by a benefit to the community. The reward is paid by the County Treasurer, under a law passed by a majority of the people in open town meeting. The farmers are always disposed to vote for a high bounty in revenge for the sheep they have lost, and the hunters because they have hope of the reward.

A man by the name of Elsworth once made a pit-fall with a bait or decoy upon it. He visited it from time to time, and on the morning of a town meeting he found in it a she-wolf with six whelps, supposed to have had their birth after the bitch had fallen in. He left them where he found them and went to the town-meeting, where he made an animated discourse upon the mischievous depredations of these ravening animals; stated in glowing colours the losses and terrors of the farmers and finished by proposing a bounty such as might encourage some enterprising spirits to devote themselves entirely, and with zeal, to their destruction. His eloquence was popular and successful. The bounty was doubled; next morning he went with a neighbor to examine his pit-fall and taking the seven scalps, claimed and received for each, the augmented recompense. The secret might have been kept till this day had not his vanity tempted him to boast of his ingenuity in "taking in the flats."

The bears are also numerous and mischievous in the new settlements. They destroy not only the corn-fields, but even the swine when they meet them in the woods; but when they are taken they pay damages, the furs being worth from four to ten dollars. Their flesh is tolerably good food, their hams when dried and smoked are preferable to smoked beef. It is a remarkable fact in which all the hunters agree that no person has yet been able to take the she-bear with young.

The panther is more wary of man, and shy of approaching his habitation. The grey, red, and cross-foxes are plenty; the martin, sable, the fisher, mink, and racoon are hunted for their furs, as are the beaver, otter, and muskrat, and produce annually a very handsome remittance.

There is an observation touching the fox and the wolf, which, though foreign from our subject may be worth your attention as a matter of curiosity, and of some interest to those who make a study of natural history. It is a common, and I believe, an uncontradicted opinion* that the dog, the fox, and the wolf are all of one species and will intermix their race. Many dogs strongly resembling wolves, are shown as instances of this and are called wolf-dogs; others of a smaller stature and bearing the characteristics of the fox are called fox dogs, and thought to be a cross-race, half fox, half dog: but after taking much pains to inquire and after many years' residence in situations where such a breed would be most likely to appear, if the nature of these animals had not forbidden it, I am fully persuaded that they do not intermix. If ever, therefore, such a fact did happen, of which I have little faith,

---

*It is evident the writer was unacquainted with the careful and minute experiments made and detailed by Buffon upon this subject; however, it is a proof of the accuracy of his observation that without any particular regard or research, he should have come to the same conclusion in contradiction of a popular opinion, universally received among the inhabitants of the country.

W. S.

it must have been rather one of those sports of nature, by which her own laws, are sometimes, though rarely violated, than the effect of any fixed or natural law; and a strong proof that it was never intended that these animals should become promiscuous is, that the wolf carries her young five weeks longer than the dog, and the fox a much shorter time.

The elk and moose-deer are found in various places, their flesh is of excellent flavor, and their hides make a strong and useful leather. Their period of gestation is nine months and they will intermix with the cow. Some persons will have as much difficulty in crediting this fact as in doubting of the other; the following is an instance which puts it past all doubt. A Mr. Hopkins of Vermont, let his cattle run on a mountainous part of that state in the summer of 1795; in the following winter he removed with his stock to Otsego; there one of his cows had a calf which bore the characters of one and the other race, and was said to be half cow, half moose. This calf grew to be a cow and had several calfs, but they were found to be unprofitable giving but little milk and being with difficulty restrained by the fences. They always inclined rather to browse up on the trees and shrubs than to feed upon the grass.

The legs of the moose are so long that without spreading their feet wide asunder they cannot bring their mouths to the ground, and evidently are not destined by nature to pasture on the grass. They travel with great rapidity, their swiftest gait being a long trot. The male is nineteen hands high having enormous horns which he casts every spring. The deer are found in abundance in every new settlement, and for the first ten years form an article of provisions in every family; their skins when dressed are used by glovers and breeches makers and often to make clothing for children.

The squirrel and the hare follow the plantations and are seldom seen far from improved lands. The martin formerly preyed upon the squirrel, but now being hunted for his fur, the latter has found in man an ally, the former an enemy. The martin, therefore, becomes every day more scarce, the squirrel more plenty; the flesh of this little animal is delicate to eat. The hare is said to be the same as the English hare, with the exception that it is smaller. The rabbit is not very plenty.

There are a number of other animals indigenous in the woods; but as they are unimportant to the farmer, neither yielding him advantage on the one hand by their flesh or their fur, nor on the other giving him any annoyance it would be wandering from our purpose to describe them.

BIRDS.

The birds which afford any profit to the farmer, are:

The wild-duck, which are of various kinds, and taken in abundance, and are useful as well for their flesh, as their feather.

The wild-goose; they are very shy however, and seldom caught; they fly very high, and pass in large flocks to the sea in the months of November and December, and return in the spring to the lakes. Their flight from the lakes is a sure warning that winter is about to set in, and their return brings notice to all the vast territories where they pass, that it is at an end. Sometimes, in heavy snow or in rain, their feathers become so drooping, and charged with wet, that they become fatigued and unable to continue their flight, light in the open fields or on small waters, and are shot.

There are many instances of a single goose stopping on her way to lay her eggs; the gander with whom she is paired, abandons the flock to remain with her; they pitch upon some small lake, pool, or creek. I have known the farmers to discover their nests on the borders of these waters, and take their eggs, and have them hatched under a tame goose; the brood will continue till the ensuing spring; towards that season, unless the owner has had care to clip their wings, they will prefer the savage state, and take their flight with the first wild flock they descry, and whose noise in the air excites their native passion for wandering.

The partridge, or as it is called with us, the pheasant, is in abundance. The quail follows the settlements, and is not plenty, but the woodcock, snipe, and plover are. The wild pigeon is extremely common, and its squab is much preferred to the young of the tame species, being equally fat, and of a higher game flavor; they breed in groves of small trees, their nests are coarsely made, and form a close neighborhood, so that sometimes thousands of them will be found together. Amongst the luxurious delicacies which the wilderness offers to the sensualist, the principle are these young squabs, taken very early; the moose's nose, the beaver's tail, and the brook trout.

The eagle is scarce, breeding seldom, but living to a great age.

The hawks are of various kinds, they are in all parts of the country, and in the new settlements are destructive to the poultry, but after a few years are generally hunted out. The owl is also destructive, and ravages the hen-roost in the night.

In the autumn, the crow, blackbird, and jay destroy the farmer's crop. I might, in speaking of the squirrels, have observed, that some of them play an active part also in this mischief, the small red and striped kind particularly.

The wood-mouse eats the seed in the spring; many means have been tried of destroying these little animals, but none have been found so efficacious as the keeping a number of cats; they will completely banish them.

Venomous serpents are but rare, and are confined to a few rocky spots. The rattle-snake is very poisonous, as every body knows, but it seldom bites, and never without warning by the rattling of its tail; the noise it makes is not much unlike the sound of the locust. Its extraordinary power of fascination is not only fatal to the wood-birds, but is exercised equally on the tame poultry and the squirrels. It is as difficult to describe the effects as to conceive the cause of this phenomenon; but it is curious to observe the progress of so strange an affection through all its gradations, from the first fluttering transports, to the moments of panting agony, and the last crisis of fatal crispation, when the victim falls breathless and motionless at the mercy of its devourer. The eyes of the serpent, whilst intent upon its victim, project and shine with unusual animation; his body exhibits various shades of burnished brightness; he generally remains coiled, with his crest erect, but motionless; but no sooner has he swallowed his prey than his brilliancy fades, and all his splendid and luxuriant coloring is succeeded by a mixture of dusky black and yellow. These snakes, however, are very rare, little feared by men, and soon disappear from a settled country; their bite, however, is attended with acute pain, the parts round the wound become swelled and spotted, and fever and delirium ensue; but I have known few to be bitten, and no one to die in consequence.

I once had a surveyor's chain-bearer bitten, but an application being made of pounded water-pepper,* (or arsesmart,) he was relieved in a few hours time.

The same herb produced a cure as speedy upon an ox, which had received a bite on the side of his head, and was greatly swollen in consequence; a poultice being tied on the part affected, in two hours time a complete cure was operated; this fact happened near Schohola. Both these instances took place under my own eyes. I learned the virtues of this useful herb from an Indian trader, and it is worthy of remark that it is generally to be found among the loose rocks where the rattle snakes haunt.

Having mentioned those animals which fall within our present sphere of inquiry, that is, such as may be considered useful or noxious to the settler, I leave the others, of which there is an endless variety, to be treated of by the curious.

As to objects of natural history, or scientific research, whether vegetables or mineral, they have never been my pursuit, and if I have departed from the course of mere practical information, it has only been when I had reason to know, or strongly to believe, that those who had undertaken to announce to the world certain facts and opinions, were themselves mistaken or misled; and have shortly noted them as matters which you or others so disposed may bestow their attention in examining. One indeed who took delight in the study of nature, and was qualified

---

*Persicaria.

to pursue her through her wonderful variety, might find in this tract of country a rich and ample field, and abundant matter for beautiful and useful description.

The oil skimmed from the surface of the springs and waters in the Allegany hills, and Seneca lake, and called Seneca oil, is well known to possess strong medical virtues. The many other medical waters, so various in their qualities and combinations, and the salt springs which supply the country with that precious article, are objects worthy of the philosopher's research.

The remains of field-works, apparently erected by ancient and powerful Indian nations, but at a period so remote that tradition does not reach it; vast fortresses or intrenched camps, sometimes covering ten acres in space, surrounded by ditches and guarded by pit-falls, artfully contrived for the destruction of an enemy; the many stone-axes, leaden pipes, spears of flint, vessels of pottery, the gritty stones on which the ancient inhabitants have sharpened their implements of labor or of war, before the use of iron had perfected the arts either of destruction or convenience; all those are still to be seen, and seem irresistibly to prove that it has been with men as with the brute creation, and that with one as with the other, in the lapse of ages, distinct races have passed away and been forgotten.

The great fall of Niagara is at once the most sublime and interesting scene of nature. On leaving New York for that place, you first sail one hundred and sixty miles up the noble river of the Hudson, whose banks present to the eye a rich variety of landscape, and an admirable contrast between the frowning terrors of forest-crowned precipices, and the cultivated abodes of industry and peace. In the course of this passage, hundreds of merchant vessels are to be seen gliding in every direction, and intersecting each other's track. The remainder of the journey is westward by land about three hundred and fifty miles. The road lies through a champaign country, rich and improved. From the number of heavy wagons, strong teams, and valuable loadings passing to market, an idea may be formed of the wealth of the country and the prosperity of its inhabitants. From the Black-rock, near

Buffalo creek, an outlet of lake Erie, you pass the straights of Niagara, in good boats, to the Canadian shore, and then proceed down the river's bank by a smooth and well-made road, through an improved and beautiful country. About fifteen miles before you arrive at the falls, the scene opens to view, and the tremendous roaring of the waters strike the ear; sometimes when the wind and the state of the atmosphere are favorable, they are heard at a much greater distance; the spray rises like a misty cloud towards the sky, and refracting the vivid beams of the sun, presents to the delighted spectator all the rich and luxuriant colors of the rainbow.

At the town of Chippaway the rapids begin, and the current becomes accelerated, descending with an inclination of about six degrees, for about three-quarters of a mile; wedge-formed rocks rise from the surface and break the smoothness of the waters. Hence the indignant foam and angry roaring which strike the senses of the traveler, and prepare his mind for the still sublimer scenes which they announce. In vain is the strength and fury of unmeasurable waters wasted upon these sturdy mounds; in vain the unremitting conflict, the destinies of nature are fulfilled. The fugitive waters pursue their vagrant course, the unshaken rocks remain emblems of the great power whose laws have made them fixed; yet time will come when they must undergo the fate of matter, and when those billows which they now dash from their sides in harmless froth shall mine their strong foundations and precipitate them from their ancient holds.

Next is the Grand-pitch—before this majestic image of eternal power the soul is fixed in awe and reverence— the voice of a companion is irksome—self is forgot—full of the idea of Almighty power—though terrible, delightful—sense dwells upon the image—thought wanders obscurely after something which it cannot grasp, and the beholder is lost in ecstacy as I am in description!

TAXES

Our taxes are so light that a rich man will readily spend more in one or two entertainments, than the amount of all his taxes; and generally his voluntary donations for benevolent and useful institutions, are ten times more than the law exacts of him; and the poor man will spend as much, unnecessarily in taverns, as the law demands of him for every public purpose. The fair average tax for a well seated farmer, on an hundred acres, is about the produce of one-sixth of an acre per annum. Large tracts of forest lands pay about twelve cents per hundred acres, more or less, according to the situation, the soil, and the wants of the country. The clergy are supported without any establishment of law, and live with decency; and the people show a great willingness to support religious institutions and generally attend places of public worship, which convinces me that neither the interference of laws nor the excitement of persecution, nor of controversy, are necessary to stimulate men to that which seems more a principle of their nature than a matter of regulation or convention.

I have often witnessed the beneficial effects of this religious disposition, and of the institutions growing out of it. The settlement of Cooperstown, as I have before stated, was made by the poorest order of men; they labored hard all the week, but on Sunday they either went a hunting or fishing, or else collected in taverns, and loitered away the day, careless of their dress or actions— the sons caught the manners of the fathers, and for the first ten years before any religious establishment was formed, the want of it was manifest. We then turned our attention to remedy this evil, and our pains were rewarded; for since that time new and better morals and manners have prevailed, and it is now become a matter of honest pride, and as it were, a fashion to be orderly and correct. If any still follow the ancient practice of fishing and hunting on a Sunday they no longer go openly and publicly, but privately and unseen. The people now appear in decent clothing; they are taught to love each other, and the pastor mixing among them, promotes by his influence and persuasion a happy spirit of union and good will. When neighbors quarrel he interposes, sooths their angry passions, gently chides the froward, points out the mischiefs that accompany contention, and exhorts them by the love of a religion, whose spirit is peace; the respect they bear his person gives weight to his reasons; they soon feel in the quiet and satisfied state of their minds the benefit of his counsels; they listen to him not as a master but a friend, and pay him a willing obedience beyond what the authority of magistrates or the power of government ever could enforce.

You have asked me what was my motive for first settling in the Wilderness; it is pretty clearly shown in my answer to your first inquiry, to have been for the sole purpose of promoting my interest; but I may also add, that after having been employed for twenty years in the same pursuit of improving lands, I am now by habit so attached to it, that it is the principal source which remains to me of pleasure and recreation.

Why I have succeeded where many others have failed, is also simple and easy to explain; they have followed plans quite opposite to mine, and fallen into all the errors I have above detailed; they have reserved favorite tracts, retained mill-sites in their own hands; they have opened expensive roads, and built costly bridges at their own charge. They have too early insisted with rigor upon payment, and forced the purchaser to surrender a part or the whole of his possession. The reserved tracts seem to proclaim that the settlement is not becoming populous or thriving. The withholding a mill-place, is depriving the people of a convenience, which they cannot want, instead of encouraging people to gather together and to undertake for their own common advantage, by their common labor, those works which their necessities first point out. When the landlord undertakes to construct buildings, bridges, and roads, and the people labor for hire, each man strives to get the most he can for the least services, so that at the end of ten or fifteen years the first cost advances, and interest upon them calculated, will leave little or no profit, and disgust and discouragement ensue.

My advice then is to fill the land with people, whether rich or poor; call them together when occasion requires to undertake some general work, where every one feels his own particular interest, and a few quarts of liquor cheerfully bestowed, will open a road or build a bridge, which would cost if done by contract, hundreds of dollars.

Sell the mill-place to a man that can build upon it, or if you should sell it to one who has not the means, furnish them to him, and make him debtor to you for the advances. He will work better and cheaper for himself than for you; you will not then be cheated, and you will have a good profit in the convenience and advantage which your settlement will derive from it.

Europeans are too apt to conceive that coming from an older and more highly improved country, their own opinions must be preferable to those of the native Americans, and they follow, without consulting the lights of experience, the practice of their own country; they first injudiciously spend the capital they brought with them, then draw for more, and after sowing much and reaping little, abandon the pursuit as hopeless. Such men, it is true, do good, but not to themselves; they leave money behind them, of which others reap the advantage; but they seldom improve their own interest as they would in a business they had understood. To have a great capital is not so necessary as to know how to manage a small one, and never to be without a little. The people will not only join in works beneficial to themselves, but they will find their own provisions; the landlord has but to appear with his keg of rum to treat them, and more manual labor will be accomplished in one day by men thus collected, than by double the number of hirelings. For all these purposes therefore it is not large funds that are wanted, but a constant supply, like a small stream that never dries.

You will probably expect from me some calculations of the cost of clearing new lands, but this is so variable, and depends upon so many accidental circumstances, that any scale of that kind would tend rather to mislead than to direct a stranger; it is, however, good to observe, that a man who is careful of his ashes, and profits by the advantage which new clear land affords, that of raising his first crop without the expense of either ploughing or weeding, is rather a gainer by the wood which he has to cut down.

If a farmer hires choppers to clear his land, it will cost him about three pounds per acre, that is, seven dollars and a half; for this money he will have the trees felled and cut into logs of fourteen feet in length, and the branches thrown together in heaps, ready for burning. If he contracts to have the whole fenced as well as cleared, the common price is ten pounds (twenty-five dollars) per acre, the farmer reserving the ashes to himself—some will get their lands cleared for the ashes and the first crop; I have, myself, given the three first crops to have the land well inclosed and fitted for the scythe; but the most usual way is to hire a farmer by the month, and for the farmer and his sons to labor with him, and then a large fallow is prepared. The ashes and the first crop, as I have stated, being thus obtained without trouble or tillage, will produce a better profit than could be obtained from the tillage of a lean soil in an old improved farm; the labor, it is true, is greater, but the profit bears a greater proportion to the labor, and richly compensates for it; and it is a general observation, that a man's profits are never greater than at the time of clearing his lands. But in every stage of the business, one dollar, in the hands of a thorough practical man, will reproduce more than ten under the management of a theorist; therefore, the European would do well, instead of following his own whims, or acting upon plans, however prudent in his own country, impracticable here, to hire a capable and experienced person for six months' time, and be governed by him in his mode of clearing, planting, sowing, and gathering his crops. It is to be observed also, that one American will clear more in a day than three Europeans. The Irish laborer excels with the spade and the flail, but is not a match for the American at other country-work: the Scotch succeed in the woods as elsewhere, being frugal, cautious in their bargains, living within their means, and punctual in their engagements; if a Scotchman kills a calf he will take the best part of it to market, and husband up the price of it; if he consumes any part at home, it will be the coarsest and the cheapest; the American will eat the best part himself, and if he sells any, will lay out the money upon some article of show; the odds are, that when the Scotchman buys a cow, he pays ready money, and has her for a lower price; the American pays with his note, gives more, and is often sued for the payment; when this happens, his cause comes to be tried before the squire, and six jurors impanelled. Here much pettifogging skill is displayed; if the defendant has address enough to procure a note, bond or other matter to be offered in set-off, he perhaps involves his adversary in costs to the amount of three or four dollars, and gains celebrity for his dexterity and finesse. This cunning talent, which they call out-witting, gives him such reputation and lead, that he stands fair to be chosen a petty town officer.

It is to be regretted that so mischievious a spirit of litigation should be encouraged by some of the justices, who, for the sake of a paltry fee, forget the great duty of their office, that of preserving peace; and that it should have increased as it has done of late years, to a shameful extent. I have known more than one hundred precepts issued in one day by some of those squires. A magistrate who becomes so ready an instrument of contention may be considered a living calamity. Some, however, I have known of a quite different stamp, who have carried the spirit of peace-making and benevolence so far, as to leave their own business and travel miles for the sake of recon-ciling parties, and putting an end to quarrels, and who sought for no other reward than the satisfaction of doing good.

Sometimes proclamations are to be seen posted up in the country inns, that by virtue of an execution issued out of the office of A. B., Esq., the cow of John, or the bed of Peter is to be sold on such a day. These notices serve at the same time to advertise the people where the office of this trader in justice is, and bring him in more practice, and more custom to the tavern; for when the day of the sale arrives, eating and drinking are of course. There those who have not money go on credit—payment is demanded—another dispute arises, and another suit is commenced—and time and money are spent, which if well employed would have added to the comfort of the family, and increased the stock of the farm.

Where religious establishments prevail there is more forbearance, and more accommodation. The magistrate catches the tone and temper of the society, and is a useful member of it. Upon such institutions then depends in a great measure the correction of the above destructive vice; and it will be the certain result of those establishments, unless the spirit of party should run too high, and prevent the election of men in authority whose motives will be the honest pride of character and the feeling of conscience and duty.

LANDS

It is difficult to point out any general rule, for the direction of a stranger in our country, as to the choice of lands. There are some, it is true, that will stand the test of experience, but the application of them cannot be easy, as they must be combined with so many circumstances of situation, climate, etc., which if not well understood and attended to, would render them deceitful and contradictory. For instance, in the eastern counties of Pennsylvania, the chestnut indicates a lean soil; whereas in the western counties of New York it is found on rich and generous land, suited entirely to the growth of wheat.

Where the bass-wood, the butter-nut, the sugar-maple, white-ash, elm, and tall red-beech is the prevailing timber, you may be certain of a good soil both for grain and grass. If it is interspersed with hemlock it is not the worse. The black-walnut is never found but in strong and durable ground.

The large topped, short mossy-beech denotes ungenerous land. The poplar in our climate promises good wheat.

The pitch-pine uniformly bespeaks a thin sandy land.

The white-pine is found in all sorts of ground; when it grows on a plain, the soil is apt to be quick and very kindly; but the stump being two or three feet in diameter will take more time to decay than the tree took to grow, owing to its resinous nature. Notwithstanding this, however, such tracts will be among the most valuable on account of the timber as I have before stated.

The alder-bush is a sign of good grass.

The many kinds of oak grow on as many kinds of soil; but the large smooth-barked black-oak is never found but on a good soil, the large, tall white-oak never but on a clay bottom.

The hickory where it is tall and thriving is a favorable symptom.

Those lands which produce spontaneously the birch and the spruce are the last taken up.

The lime-stone is the truest of all indications, and that which never will deceive the man who is in quest of a profitable farm. Lime-stone land is good in all situations.

The gray-stone is generally a good token, but wherever it is round, oval, and smooth, like what is called the cobbler's lap-stone, apparently water-worn, that soil will be sterile.

To an attentive and practiced observer, the running waters will afford instruction. If the course of the little brook is lively, and the water in time of freshets, or the sediment deposited by them be of a light chocolate color, loose and loamy, it proves that that water has passed through a good tract of country. Whereas if the water wear a whitish appearance, and there be many large round stones, that brook must have had its course through a poor tract. If it appears black, it heads in a tamarack or spruce swamp, but may pass through much good land, which can always be discovered by the little banks and shoals formed by its deposits as above mentioned.

Those tracts of country which hold the water on their surface, are neither so healthy for man, nor so sure for crops as a free and loamy soil.

When a great tree is cut down in the poor clay-ground, and happens to fall upon smaller ones, if they break under its weight, it is a proof that the ground is hard and poor; or if instead of breaking they be forced up by the roots, the roots will be found large and much earth will adhere to them. But where the tree turns up a small root, there the ground is loose and good.

These observations only apply to that soil where there is, a little below the surface, a stratum of cold or metallic concretion: for there are some clays which will at all times yield the heaviest crops of wheat, particularly in a drisly or dripping season. These clays will hold manure longer than any other soil. But the clay, generally speaking, fails in a dry season.

The three ingredients which when they combine form the most productive of all soils, are the lime-stone, the chocolate-loam, and dark-brown sand. Ground so composed will bear rain and drought; is certain and durable.

There is a kind of clay which approaches very near to marble, and is common in the Genesee country, the counties of Seneca, Cayuga, Jefferson, and St. Lawrence, and the west part of Clinton; it is of a loose quality, plants take good root in it, and grow of a darker green than in ordinary soils. The wheat raised on those lands has less bran, and makes whiter flour than that raised on the mere loam.

Stony land is less agreeable to cultivate, but there are some stony tracts that turn out very advantageous; and the nature of the stone as above stated may be a guide to the choice.

There is an advantage in having the stone, when necessary, for fencing and building; and as the stony land retains the moisture, it is better for grass and for fruit-trees.

Wherever land produces good natural grass, it will not be easily worn out in tillage. The natural grass of the country we are treating of, is white clover, or honeysuckle, which shows itself spontaneously very soon after the sun beams have been let to shine upon the earth. It is the bed of pasture, but not profitable to mow in a rough bottom, which all new lands must have. The farmer therefore prefers timothy, and clover which grows as high as three feet: then though the scythe should leave a stubble of six inches, a plentiful crop is still gathered in. After the land has been ploughed and leveled the white clover can be mown, and is the best hay.

HOME MANUFACTURES, AND RAW MATERIALS

Throughout this tract of country the wife and daughter of the farmer spin and weave their own bed clothing, and common wearing apparel. The cloth they make is about three-quarters of a yard wide, and very stout. They comb part of the wool, and manufacture a worsted cloth for petticoats and gowns. They also make a strong durable checkered cloth for aprons. When the fleeces are shorn, about the twentieth of May, the mistress sets apart the best for stockings, and the next best for the clothing of her husband and sons; the rougher wool is made into blankets. The quality of the fleeces depends much, as you must know, upon the keeping of the sheep, and the care bestowed upon them. The average quantity is about three pounds when washed; though some sheep will yield seven, and some, but very rarely, as much as ten.

We produce a partial supply of iron for our own consumption. The ore is found in many places, but from want of knowledge in working our mines, few attempts have yet been made in that most important of all manufactures, and the Western country is obliged to pay large sums annually for a material with which it abounds. No article meets a more rapid sale, and no establishment is so much wanted, or so ardently desired as that of iron-foundries. In Nobleborough and Arthurborough there are specimens of the richest ore found in the close vicinity of populous and flourishing settlements, with constant streams and plentiful falls, and inviting situations for mills of every kind.

In most of the Western counties, however, are made the best of scythes, hoes, and some other implements of husbandry, adapted to the purposes of the country for which they are intended. Those imported from England are useless here, and therefore no person coming from your country with a view to settle, should bring with him any farming utensils, or mechanics' tools, except those which I shall now specify: let him bring cross-cut saws, hand-saws, hand-mill saws, planes of all kinds, chisels, turning tools, and trace chains. It is true we can make all these, but as yet we do not make them either so cheap or so good as those that come from Europe.

The manufactures of leather, wool, fur-hats, and common earthen-ware are all flourishing. That of leather, where bark is so plenty, ought of course to prosper, but as the cattle are mostly driven to the sea ports, the hides are lost to the country manufacturer. If the beef was barreled and salted in the country this inconvenience would be remedied, and the encouragement would be greater, and the profit would be more to the farmer, but these things are never to be forced. And in a part of the world where the minds of men are so unshackled, and where they are not certainly dull-sighted to their own interest, there is little fear that they will not find it out. The facility of carriage by the increase of turnpike-roads, and inland navigations will operate to that end, and the increasing wealth and prosperity of the country will complete it.

The manufacture of window-glass near Albany is already sufficient for the consumption of the country, and comes as cheap, and is as good as the British.

Oil is made from flax-seed in most of the Western counties.

ABSURDITIES

You have desired to know the causes of so many failures by enterprisers in new lands, and I have, under their respective divisions, pointed out several. I shall now take a more general view of that subject, and conclude my correspondence with a relation of the principal absurdities which have fallen under my observation, and which have been the causes of bad success.

An Irish gentleman, of fortune, purchased a large tract. Full of ideal superiority, and high-minded enterprise, he cast his eyes around him, and interpreted all he saw into proofs of the weakness of our uncultivated minds. His plans were instantaneously formed, and he enjoyed, by confident anticipation, the pleasure of self-aggrandizement; the glory of rescuing a people from the empire of ignorance, and, I dare say, the generous pride of doing good. He sent home for such objects as he conceived instrumental to his success; he got a supply of tackles, blocks, windlasses, and capstans, with other mechanical auxiliaries. With these, and a number of men, he went to work—he pulled down the trees by force of men and machines—some he broke, some he overturned by the roots; but in order to effect this, he often spent five times more labor, independent of his mechanic powers, in barely chopping through the spreading roots, than would have served at first to have hewn down the tree. His pride forbade him to recede, and he succeeded in clearing a few acres at an enormous expense. I foresee that you will applaud him at least for having got rid of those stumps and roots which encumber, and in the eye of a European, so much disfigure the face of the soil; but I can assure you, that the deep caverns made by this violence, and the great quantities of cold and barren earth which these roots brought up with them, burying and impoverishing the rich layer of mould and ashes which are the encouraging reward of the settlers' first toils, were a much greater evil than all the stumps and roots, if suffered to remain; besides it is next to impossibility to roll those monstrous roots together, so as to be consumed by fire, damp as they must be, and covered with masses of earth. You are more puzzled how to get quit of them, after laboring to bring them above ground, than you were before to dispose of the whole tree; and that especially in a country where the poorest laborer will, in the shortest day, receive half a dollar for his work, over and above his provisions. At length this gentleman found out that it was one thing to dress his pleasure grounds in Ireland, and another to clear the Wilderness in America, and finished by admitting that in matters of husbandry experience was a better guide than either fancy or philosophy, and that none were more capable than those whom practice had made proficients.

Another Irish gentleman purchased a larger tract, and brought with him a number of his own tenants—his patent kitchen, his huntsmen, his hounds, his fishing apparatus, with workmen, and all that he supposed fit provision for founding a large establishment. He did not forget hampers of good claret, so necessary to give wisdom to a young beginner; perhaps, sir, this latter failing is not that for which you will be inclined to censure him too severely. During three summers he *toiled* in this manner, and never raised ten bushels of grain, nor one hundred weight of hay; but he expended in the country about twelve hundred pounds of Irish money and then bid adieu to his farm, and to the Western hemisphere.

An Englishman by the name of Ockley purchased a farm of me—he scoffed at our Yankee mode of clearing away the trees—he also sent for his ropes, his tackle-falls, and his pulleys; he sent moreover for leathern girdles, with buckles and straps, and furnished his workmen with mallets and polished chisels. Either he or his man would climb to the top of the highest tree and there fix his purchase; then another man below girded himself round with a girth that had stirrup leathers and stirrups attached to it, and was hoisted up by a rope; to this rope was also fixed a basket of tools, and the workman and his tools were thus pulled up about a hundred feet high. There he began his operations by sawing off the top of the tree above the seizing of his block; this done he was lowered down from limb to limb, sawing away branch after branch. When, however, the branches encumbered each other, so that his saw would not work, he took out his mallet and chisel, stood up in his stirrups and chiseled away. So he proceeded for one entire summer, and during the time that the heat was on him it would have been impertinent, if not dangerous, to advise him. He had come from a country distinguished for agricultural improvement, and could not look but with disdain upon our infant arts. Our counsels he considered as the lessons of a school-boy to his preceptor. He did not break his neck, but he destroyed his fortune, and bade farewell to the woods, leaving no other representatives behind than thousands of bare poles, resembling nothing so much as the masts of dismantled shipping in a harbor.

There was another English gentleman who would not condescend to cut down a tree but with an English axe, nor plough but with a heavy English plough. He would not sow seed till every stump was first grubbed up; and it seemed his chief maxim to do nothing as the Americans did; of this he was so punctillious an observer that he shocked his wheat with the heads downward, because, he said, the ground would take the rankness out of the grain. The crop of several acres stood in shock, in wet weather, during ten or twelve days, and in that position began to grow, more to the amusement of his neighbors, than to his profit, and he remains to this day obstinate and poor.

Whilst I make free with the errors of others, let me not be supposed to glorify in myself. I have committed follies which I have not forgot. When I went first into the woods I was as bigoted to the methods I had been used to observe in Pennsylvania, as these Europeans were to theirs. I would not sow till the saplings were first grubbed up, and I ploughed the ground for the first crop, not considering that the immense quantity of timber to be burned consumed all the small roots and of itself prepared the ground for seed; and I thought that those who did otherwise must do so from ignorance. I found fault with their fences—I caviled at the construction of their wagons, and their gear—I condemned their tools and farming implements—I talked much and to little purpose—they continued their own practices, and I found, after some time, that I had nothing better to do than to conform; and am every day more convinced, that wherever men's minds are uncontrolled they will in a short time discover what is for their interest better than strangers can instruct them; and that in countries where their actions are free, what is most in use will be found to be pretty nearly what is best; and chiefly in what concerns husbandry, and all its instruments. I can say little of other countries, having not been a traveler in them, but my own practice and observation have taught me that the people without the aid of philosophers and projectors understand their business pretty well.

Gradual improvements are made, and will grow out of experience, and certainly I am not an enemy to ingenious speculations, nor even to theories, provided they be the result of long and attentive observation, and grounded upon facts well ascertained. I only mean to say that, within the scope of my observation, I never could see that the practical farmer had derived much advantage from the meditations of the closet; and whatever experiments it may be thought useful by the learned to make, I should not wish them made at the expense of any one whose bread depended on their success. As yet I think it safer that the philosopher should learn from the farmer, than the farmer from the philosopher.

Your remarks upon those authors who have treated of the agriculture of our country are probably well founded, and were I to judge from the few specimens I have happened to see, I should say they were very just. Before a man attempts the history of any subject, he ought to know it well; and those who undertake to write upon the economy of a country would do well to wait till they had been long enough in one place to forget the many prejudices they had brought with them; and if their object be truly to instruct, they should endeavor to do it by example, which is the strongest lesson; and they will be readily followed if they can once show to those in whose interest they take concern, that they have known how to manage their own.

As to those western counties of New York, which I have been describing, they are chiefly peopled from the New England states, where the people are civil, well-informed, and very sagacious; so that a wise stranger would be much apter to conform at once to their usages than to begin by teaching them better.

W. C.